T0380176

Feeling Free

A MEMOIR

Freed from ritualistic abuse

How to forgive the unforgivable

SARAH BRAYDON

Feeling Free

A memoir about being freed from ritualistic abuse and learning how to forgive the unforgivable

Balboa Press books may be ordered through booksellers or by contacting:

Balboa Press
A Division of Hay House
1663 Liberty Drive
Bloomington, IN 47403
www.balboapress.com
1 (877) 407-4847

ISBN: 978-1-9822-1820-1 (sc)
ISBN: 978-1-9822-1821-8 (e)

Print information available on the last page.

Balboa Press rev. date: 01/26/2019

BALBOA
PRESS
A DIVISION OF HAY HOUSE

To Little One

Contents

Fabric of My Memoir 1

An Invitation 3

The Beginning of Feeling Free 5

Turning the Darkness Outward and Exposing the Living Light from Deep Within 72

Reflections 74

Profound Gratitude 81

Resources to Order by Sarah 82

Suggested Readings 83

With your permission, as the reader, I desire to delicately touch your heart
and softly speak to that profound part of you called grace.

To my beloved reader, I tell you this story, not to hurt or cause harm, not to generate fear, or not to create conflict. My purpose in writing this book is to expose and begin a discussion in order to design a powerful yet tender movement, that together we can stop this abuse. We can live freely and breathe a sigh of relief to ensure safety for all people.

This book is for survivors, relations, friends, therapists and other social workers, general readers, and those who are still caught and can't seem to break free. This is for the children who cry alone and have lost their hearts and trust. This book is for everyone.

Even if just one little wisp of tenderness and understanding is dusted by you and reaches the stars, it will bring help and hope.

There is hope.

Thank you for picking up a copy of this book. Thank you for even just glancing through it. Thank you for listening to your heart and taking it home.
The purpose of my passionate calling is that this book has
a message for you at a very enlightened level.

Fabric of My Memoir

It is the fabric of my life I would like to share and gift to you in an easy, caring, and most vulnerable way that I know how.

This fabric's tapestry is simply a complex, threaded portion of my life. I feel honored and at peace to write my story and present it to you with open arms and kind hands.

In reverence of this fabric, the complexities lie within each simple word, as if they are sewn together by the threads of understanding that my story of childhood truly reveals a deeper message. It is for those who wish to listen and feel each word in their heart.

The ones who interlaced the threads of this story may have heard, seen, or even recalled a different event. They may also remember a conversation in a different time and place, as according to the interpretation of their perception and significance.

The core of my message stands not by fear, but by hope, love, survival, and freedom. I remain steadfast and strong within my purpose and passion to reveal this fabric's message as related in my childhood story.

> " *Trust the intensely rich fiber of your own soul to guide you.* "
>
> —Joan Tarpley (author)

I gift to you, straight from my own heart's pulsation, a story of my childhood and how today I can now finally see and feel rays of sunshine on my face. As I delicately write, word by word, tears caress my cheeks. I can only wish in my dreams that you will merely listen and ask questions. Maybe, just maybe one day, one of my tears will touch one of yours. Together we can hug and share in a way that is not so far-reaching as to lead us on the path toward hope and freedom.

Perhaps you will experience a calling that is so deep within you that it propels you to speak and break the silence that was trapped and knotted inside the fabric of your own life. Untangle and loosen the knots, allowing you to finally breathe and walk forward in courage, self-love, and truth. The truth really does set you free. Now is the time, if you wish.

> *The way ahead is clear and free. I give myself permission to move out of the past with gratitude and into a joyous new day.*

—Louise L. Hay (spiritual leader, publisher, author, and speaker)

An Invitation

The messages inside this book are an invitation specifically for you. I have come to believe that everyone's personal story has a unique storyline for you to absorb. The contents of my book are perfectly placed in order for you to learn and feel a shift in your own personal life.

Perhaps the entire story will be your connection to this personal shift. It could be a small sentence that awakens a part of you that you concealed because you were confused about an aspect in your life. Whatever it is—an aha moment, a feeling, a realization, or a piece of your puzzle that fits into the empty space—what you felt was void.

I will reveal my experience carefully and calmly so you can stay with me and become aware. Perhaps you are a survivor or one who is questioning his or her memories. So then when you are reading these pages, please read softly, reflect, and then process from your heart and your own truth. Each page purposely brims with rooted hope. No matter what happens, there is always a chance to believe and plant the seed of kindness.

I have compiled other written materials besides this book that you can refer to in the back reference section. If you are seeking further guidance and opportunities for more details, just connect with me. I have developed a website with these materials that steps further inside the experiences you will read in this book.

If you are a support person or therapist, I graciously encourage your understanding, respect, compassion, listening, and intent belief. You are a vital part of this journey when someone is walking through healing abuse. Stay with us, and be present so you can learn how to touch the life of the amazing person you are supporting in an immersed, better understanding, and more informed way.

> 66 *To the world you may be one person,*
> *but to one person you may be the world.* 99
>
> Anonymous

Inquiry

As a reader, will you continue to read this book? As a reader, will you believe my story? As a reader, will you want to help? Will you sense a calling or feel a gentle pull at your heart to do something concerning what I am about to expose and speak about?

The Beginning of Feeling Free

It is time to reveal my heart and truth—to share and open wide, to create a clarity for others who were and maybe still are being abused in this manner.

I have spoken publicly at several conferences for survivors and therapists; however, I have not presented locally or in a regulated published book format. My fifteen years (1993–2008) of my healing journey have led me to a transcendence and a freeing of my life and breath.

As you read and I write, we can do this together as supporters. I can hold your hand while we gather close to our hearts in comfort. Will you listen and ask questions or just remain quiet? It is okay to remain quiet as the reader in order to reflect and connect with your feelings.

This is written through my personal experience of releasing and healing. I dip into different aspects of my childhood, adolescence, and adult life and weave in these experiences throughout this book. I do not have many childhood memories between the abuse, yet the ones I do recall I will share with you. The explanations of why I don't have these memories becomes quite clear, and I also will share the reasons why I can't remember.

When I was in my early thirties, I started to notice I was encountering difficulties in several areas of my life. Here is just a sampling of some challenges I was exhibiting:

1. Numbness of not only my feelings but my body as well, yet hypervigilant (constantly concerned for my safety)

2. Loneliness and abandonment issues
3. Constant dissociation (out-of-body sensation)
4. Extreme fatigue
5. Placing myself in unsafe conditions or just isolating myself
6. Not interested in sexual intimacy.
    a. Or if I had sex, I would dissociate and didn't care.
7. Not speaking and being considered an extremely shy person
8. Scared of everything and everybody
9. Relationship challenges with men and women
10. Not trusting anybody
11. Eating disorder and not being able to clearly see my body
12. Strange dreams and more

I only recalled a few childhood memories and in fact observed blocks of years of no memories at all. I would view childhood photos but would have no feelings or recollections about them. It was as if I saw another child in the photos. "That was not me! I don't remember!"

I wrote in one of my many old journals, "Feeling depressed/not wanting to be here. What's wrong with me? I feel like I want to scream! What's wrong?"

I decided in my early thirties to enter therapy and uncover why this was going on inside of me. It was an expensive journey, yet I knew I needed help and some questions answered.

Bit by bit in a slow, intricate way, therapy started to break my protective, covered shell into tiny pieces. Many of these broken pieces contained sharp, painful shards and edges. I discovered that my feelings were now being released. For the first time in my thirty-year-old life, I started to feel safe and gained an understanding. I experienced tears, realizations, and more tears as my life puzzle was being pieced together. A deeper understanding emerged of why I was numb and dissociative. Feeling tired, lonely, and devoid of healthy emotions, I was confused and needed to gain some clarity. Insights surfaced into how my past contaminated my present. I was unhappy because I didn't know or never learned how to be happy. I didn't know how to take on the day and to feel or even look for a tiny particle of joy.

I uncovered through my memory flashbacks and frightful dreams that I was sexually, physically, emotionally, psychologically, and spiritually abused as a child and a young teenager. Apparently I had classic textbook symptoms but with some confusing issues coming forward through my flashbacks or memories. I was visioning black-hooded capes, fires, animals, blood, and screaming children, and a series of more disturbing images surfaced.

"Can't Breathe"

(1995)

Tears bubbled with memories.

Tears blackened my madness.

Tears staining, dripping with pain—

Tears of anger, anxiety and hurt.

Drowning . . .

Death . . .

No air . . .

Can't breathe.

This experience wasn't just verbal, emotional, or physical abuse. It wasn't even just sexual abuse. Usually when I mention this form of abuse, people shrink away due to the horror of it all. Some shake their heads in disbelief; others bow their heads in silence. I want to speak about it gently so you are present and aware of the words I place carefully upon these pages.

I have witnessed the darkness in many shapes and forms. Satanic abuse sounds so fifteenth century, horrible and unbelievable. But it is still occurring. We are so sophisticated that we don't want to believe it, so we keep the secret even from ourselves because it truly exists. No longer can we keep this secret, especially during these times of great shifting.

I'm wondering what would happen if the story is told? What would happen if it wasn't told? The price of keeping this secret is paid in terms of emotional, mental, physical, energetic, and spiritual disease or "dis-ease." We pay the price in entering abusive relationships with ourselves and others, addictions, spiritual annihilations, and cultural despair. We pay the price in losing our sense of compassion as well as our ability to show empathy and to connect with our true emotions.

We close our eyes. We pull up the blinders and don't want to see it. It must now be fully revealed and exposed in order for it to be dismantled. It is not my intention to leave you in horror or shock. I only want to bring awareness so you can be consciously aware. The end result of this book is to help us all claim our true selves. Perhaps what I've written sounds familiar to you, so some healing will shift into your heart. Therefore, it will gently confirm to help you touch and ignite a strength within your own self.

During the recovery phase of my life, I started to release unbelievable memories or flashbacks that would leave me questioning myself. I would think I was creating or making up these horrific pictures and feelings of terror. I would believe I was crazy. Yet only through releasing hundreds of flashbacks and each one in such detail was I enabled to hear, see, taste, feel, touch, and smell every movement and event during this form of childhood abuse.

Some days were so overpowering in dissociation, fear, and pain, which hurt like open wounds. My body and myself exhaustively swept away my breath of life. When I was releasing or expelling memories, I would experience body memories. This means that my body would feel the pain of what happened to me when the abuse took over my body as a child.

I felt sick, and it was so hard. It would be an honor if I could share my poetry of my inner emotional expression with you. The poems are scattered throughout the contents of the book and were written during my healing recovery. Please read them in knowing that I share them to help anyone in any way possible. "I'm Cold" conveys the feeling of not being safe and my inability to sleep at that time in my life.

"I'm Cold"

(1996)

Sheets are tucked.

I feel cold, not warm,

not protected from the

perpetrator.

Can't sleep.

I'm cold; my imagery reappears.

I need to be free, alone from these

blackened thoughts.

I feel cold, unprotected.

Help me; protect me . . .

Somebody.

Just as I was about to give up, an ancient, wise, esoteric light inside of me sparkled brightly. Then through the gentle and specialized guidance of several therapists, I was determined to finally be able to scramble my life together after so many unanswered questions and fervent confusion. I was also told that for several years I had been suffering from post-traumatic stress disorder (PTSD).

This made complete sense to me. If you notice within yourself any of the symptoms I unearthed from my own personal observations as an individual who was suffering from PTSD, I strongly suggest you seek assistance. Once you start receiving help, a feeling of ease begins to carefully melt you into a peaceful stance.

For over twenty years now, I tried to write this book and then would put it down and would finally start again, all the while experiencing tears of fear—fear of being ostracized and criticized, fear of not being believed, and fear of losing friendships, my integrity, and my job. I had a fear of being called crazy!

There came a point that is right now, this very moment, when I felt not a slight nudge but a strong push to share my story as a survivor of satanic abuse. These pages are filled with my vision as I could clearly see it, page by page, through my own self-reflection. Something inside of me initiated a calling to share, to expose, and to bring hope to others who have also survived. Some are still held as victims or caught and twisted inside the abuse, much like a hostage. Others are being mistreated and misunderstood by not only themselves, but by therapists, medical professionals, and society. Lives have been lost and destroyed because of the direct cause of satanic abuse. This saddens my heart and opens my soul to a purpose of "let's gently talk about this."

Through these pages, you may want to read some of the words and then put the book down and reflect or give pause. The slow movement of the book's words are intentional, and yet each word has been exquisitely placed in order for you to read and follow on a very real level.

You may even have questions about your own childhood, whereby you have missing pieces, blank spaces, sparse descriptions of events and places, or unrecalled years. Or perhaps you just can't remember a lot of your childhood. Or you have a feeling that something was "off" and are possibly experiencing strange dreams of childhood memories.

> *Perhaps the words are not strong enough, soft enough and I could have said it all better and described better. I believe I have done all I could to prevent it from being cheapened or stifled.*
>
> —Elie Wiesel (writer, professor and Holocaust survivor)

I was born in 1963 and raised in a small town in Ontario, Canada, during which time approximately four hundred people lived there. My family's business was operating a simple local store adorned with everything from fresh local foods to shampoo. My father was raised in this town and created his life within the confines of this village. He was married to my mother, a schoolteacher.

I was the eldest of three siblings. It was a typical layout for a family of three children, a dog, and a pet bird. I was raised in a village in the middle of farmed country scenes—pristine rolling hills, forests, ponds, wildlife, fields of corn and grains, wide open skies, and raw gravel roads.

The village contained one of everything: bank, hardware store, local hotel bar, restaurant, grocery store, post office, hairdresser, gas station, elementary school, and a couple churches (Catholic and Protestant).

This village, to a passerby, would present itself as a quaint whispering village. However, underneath the pinnings of the town was satanic abuse. My memories of my childhood and adolescence are scattered, as stated previously, to the point where there are several years I have no memory at all. Amnesia was the coping system. This is reflected as a form of blocking system that children create in order to deal with abuse or any form of trauma. This is a common strategy that children use to cope with such perils.

When I started my inner healing journey of self-recovery, my memories of abuse emerged. As a child, I would dissociate from my body and view the abuse out of my body. Oftentimes during the abuse, I would displace myself on the ceiling of the room and view the abuse from the ceiling. Through therapy, I started to understand that dissociation was a coping skill for my tiny girl body to deal with such atrocities.

I knew as a child that the abuse was wrong, but I couldn't do anything about it. They were adults, and I was just a little girl. There is a special spark in all children that discloses to them that a certain touch from anybody is either good or not good.

Being abused by family members and then the abusers through satanic rituals were combined as one. Being raised through satanic abuse eventually broke me in half. This form of abuse started when I was born and continued through my teens. During which time, I then left for university, in hopes to gain a basic degree. However, this didn't happen.

By the time I left for post-secondary school, I had no intact feelings, was extremely dissociative (which means I lived out of my body), felt lost in a damaged way, and couldn't understand most of my life. I felt different from everyone around me. I was scared. I felt invisible, scathed, and shut down. I stumbled through my first year of university, only to be debarred, which means my average mark for all subjects or classes was 45 percent. I was asked to leave university and was excluded. And the door closed behind me. I am alone again, feeling dark and dumped upon. Darkness upon me. Not sure why?

I believed I had failed. I went into the darkest depths of sadness and depression. I decided to live with my mother's parents, my grandparents, who were not involved with satanic abuse and lived farther away from my hometown. My father's parents were very much part of the ancient satanic abuse ceremonies. He was raised with this abuse and was so conditioned or programmed inside of the rituals. Bringing my mother into these conditions was devastating for her.

I do recall her desperately crying and saying to my brothers and I that she would drive us away to escape this abuse and live with our grandparents. Unfortunately that never happened. She was tangled, pulled, threatened, and caught, much like a fly in a spider web. Yet she always said this to us, and I held hope that one day she would drive us there. Somehow she kept me hoping, wishing, and dreaming that one day I would be free.

> *A Misty Morning Does not Signify A Cloudy Day.*

—Ancient proverb

Within about twelve years later at the age of eighteen, I actually ended up living with these "good" grandparents from my mother's side. I was there because I decided to attend college in the area and to take some easy classes for one year and then later reapply to the same university I was debarred from. Now I had a career change in mind and decided I wanted to become a teacher. Living with them was an important step on my path toward wellness and feeling whole again.

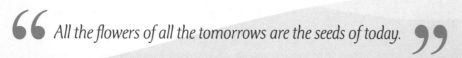

> *All the flowers of all the tomorrows are the seeds of today.*

—Anonymous

My grandmother, Mia Elizabeth, was an incredible artist. She blessed the viewers' eyes with her oil paintings. Still life, houses, country scenes, and my favorites were her flower paintings. The flowers were freshly collected from her ocean of flower gardens.

> *And the day came when the risk to remain tight in the bud was more painful than the risk it took to blossom.*
>
> —Anais Nin (novelist)

Each wave in these "flower oceans" shone forth like a cascading rainbow of colors, glistening from the hundreds of petite petals that appeared to be singing in joy from her cultivating, care-taking love.

> *It is at the edge of a petal that love waits.*
>
> —William Carlo Williams (poet and pediatric physician)

She graced me by her teachings of how to paint with oil paints and draw with skinny charcoal and pencil. She taught me her special technique of how to mix colors and apply to the paper and wood canvas with ease and enchantment. Still to this very day, I give gratitude to my grandmother. She was an absolute, patient angel for me during my confusing, young life. She was my saving grace. She crossed over in 1992, and I do remember feeling an intense feeling of calmness in her death. I often see and feel her Spirit in the depths of my soul.

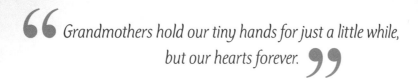

I still could not explain all of my continued symptoms. I asked myself, "Why am I not happy? Why do I not have any true friends? Why do I not date?" When I graduated university in 1987 with a four-year honors degree, I was strong in my mind and thinking, but void of any feelings. This is typical when your emotions are shut down. Your mind quickly takes over.

After I graduated from university, I was quickly hired at a well-known pediatric hospital in a larger city. I worked on several wards, and many of the children I worked with sadly perished due to their illness. I had no sensation or feelings about their deaths. I was numb, and I realized that something was actually dead inside of me as I was empty of any emotions.

My therapy and recovery started early in the 1990s when I moved out of the larger city. I had then relinquished my position at the hospital and wished to live in a smaller city in order to practice teaching children with special needs. As stated earlier, I had almost reached thirty years of age and still remained empty and stagnant inside. I am relaying this to you as the reader in case it can help you in any possible way.

The next part of what I am about to disclose will be heard as quite horrifying. It is time we start to awaken to this form of abuse in order to expose it, so it will extinguish and become extinct. It is paramount now to loosen ego and expose all that is hidden in the shadows.

Ego is currently being dismantled, and a realignment to our true selves is becoming apparent. For this to happen, we need to be aware of the dirt in the room in order to clean it. Through exposing satanic abuse, we release and dismantle it, and it then dissolves and leaves only your true light of yourself. This is your original self, comprised of love. It means breaking free and finding what you need in order to be free. I needed to release so I could feel emotion and live freely without fear.

The primary focus of satanic abuse is to teach ego and to program and stack programs of fear into the members of satanic worship and those they abuse.

You could consider fear as a created illusion, aiming to assert itself and attempting to make itself more real than love. Love is our true essence of being, combining togetherness and Oneness. Fear or ego consists of separation, competition, and greed, and it contains lies.

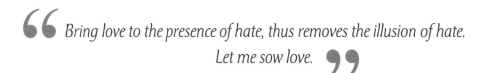

Bring love to the presence of hate, thus removes the illusion of hate. Let me sow love.

—Anonymous

The satanic programs try to convince you into thinking that all the fearful thoughts you have are yours that hide in your personality, and they attempt to make you believe that you created them and therefore you are an awful person. I was programmed to believe I was unworthy, messed up, and self-loathing, and then I continued to create just more of the same.

This unworthiness feeds off the energy of fear, which attracts more negative feelings and thoughts. Being raised in a satanic abuse environment is truly different from other forms of abuse because of the satanic programming, which involves mind controlling and the bending and distortion of your thoughts in opposite directions.

A great book by Richard Brodie, author and speaker, called *Virus of the Mind* (Hay House 1996) speaks about planting ideas and mind viruses or memes through conditioning and programming thoughts. According to Brodie, a meme is a "unit of information in a mind whose existence influences events, in other words, producing more copies of itself that become created in other minds."

Another term to use is "mind infections." These all stem and are rooted from ego beliefs or <u>E</u>dging <u>G</u>race <u>O</u>ut or <u>E</u>dging <u>G</u>od <u>O</u>ut. I like to look at the word FEAR as <u>F</u>alse <u>E</u>xpectations <u>A</u>ppearing <u>R</u>eal.

> " *Try not to let your fears sway the soft and gentle murmurings of your beautiful heart. We are immortal, eternal spirits and we're always loved. In fact, we are love.* "
>
> —Anonymous

The ritualistic satanic abusive ceremonies imprint fear, and they care nothing for your well-being but instead add to your confusion and try to subtract from your fulfillment. This is their objective and intent. It's all ego based.

> " *The "distinction—memes" you may be programmed with, control information you perceive. This makes reality look different to you.* "
>
> —Richard Brodie

Deprogramming mind programs is a necessity on many levels when healing from ritualistic abuse. It is essential and frees your mind and your whole self from false teachings that are focused on hurt and pain. When I was experiencing memory flashbacks, it was important that I engage in a therapeutic intervention of deprogramming the programs accompanying the flashback memories. The programs are all related to any form of self-harm. These false core beliefs needed to be exposed, released, and healed, followed by a reversal of my perception of myself and then a remembering of my true self, which is love.

> " *There's only one of us here: What we give to others, we give to ourselves. What we withhold from others, we withhold from ourselves. In any moment, when we choose fear instead of love, we deny ourselves the experience of Paradise.* "
>
> —Marianne Williamson (spiritual teacher and author)

May I entrust with you, as I impart, just some of my experiences as a child and continue through to adolescence? The sharing of such information is presented for the purpose of exposure and awareness. I apologize for this and any form of hurt it may surface or trigger inside of your own life. However, we can now no longer hide and say it doesn't happen. Because it does. This very moment you are reading this, a child may be living through satanic abuse, and we must somehow step forward and say, "This can't happen anymore." I invite you to recite the following quotation with your hands lovingly placed on your heart before you read the next part of this book.

> We are peace, we are love, and we are still and solid in that which we know to be true. We fervently send this love to those who are presently being abused. We gift them grace, blessings, peace, and hope.

I have had detailed memories and numerous scenes that appeared to me of being tortured, burned, and group raped. I've had electrodes placed on my minute girl body. I've been locked in a box for discipline and forced to eat animal organs. I was placed in a hole in the ground and smeared with feces. I was photographed naked as an adolescent with a black bag over my head. I was drugged, placed in a coffin of blood, and threatened for my life. I was forced to watch the horrors of torture and abuse of other children, adolescents, and adults in sadistic ways. The torture involves animals, objects, specific symbols and music, chants, lotions, altars, smells, needles, and so much more.

I had to fight for my life as a child. I have visited hell and know what that is. This darkness felt so solid black and inescapable. There seemed to be no light for me. What it meant for me was to simply just live, and if I am living and breathing, I am okay.

> I couldn't see anything. I didn't understand anything. I just didn't know why this was happening. I hurt so very much as a child. Then the pain would numb, and then I could go on.

I know what it feels like to be triggered by almost anything. *Triggered* means hysteria, anxiety, panic attack, and fear, then followed by disassociation or a numbing out.

I was triggered by certain words, smells, jewelry, tools, needles, times of day, body postures, physical touch (massage therapy was impossible especially with oils), sexual intimacy, tones, and sounds (chants and forms of music). And various foods would trigger me. Challenging times and occasions for me were birthdays, Halloween, Christmas, first day of school, and, above all, Easter. The reason being is that some actual holidays and other specific dates were times of heightened ritualistic ceremonies, and I would be triggered with anxiety during these calendar times. As I was delving inside the terrifying memories of abuse, I began to piece my life together, and explanations started to arrive.

One of my turning points in my healing of the triggers was to actually feel the specific point of time when I started to "begin to dissociate." To be aware and present, inside of the beginning of this feeling, is most vital in one's journey through abuse. It was the key that took me on a path of discovery, placement, and realization, and then came the healing.

For example, when I was listening to chanting music, I was learning to understand the exact moment I would begin to dissociate. I now had developed the coping strategies to understand the feelings of fear attached to the chanting music. I learned how to release these feelings and then calm myself down.

Working through hundreds of triggers and knowing how to deal with these triggers set me even further into a life of freedom. I worked hard with my inner girl child and walked hand in hand with her, every step of the way. Some of my most profound healing work was integrating my inner child to my adult-safe, woman-self. Eventually my inner child felt safe and at last felt loved by me! We were now integrated as one.

The cult used all of my senses to program and mind control me. I started to understand why I was triggered by so much in my life. I comprehended why I had experienced difficulties when confronted with seeing black- and red-caped robes, along with being in churches, older buildings, and barns. These were the locations where the satanic abuse occurred as well as in various basements, community halls, and certain church camps. I have several detailed memories of the abuse occurring in the village's local Catholic Church.

The black-caped robes are a common form of clothing that is worn during the ceremonies as well as the red-caped robe. Every single aspect in satanic worship and abuse has a specific meaning and symbolism or representation.

I have had challenges eating certain foods such as red meat, soups, stews, and other types of foods. During my recovery and even prior to, I was exhibiting patterns of eating disorders whereby I would only eat licorice and chocolate. They would act as laxatives and give me the ability to at least control something in my life. As my recovery deepened, I developed strategies to grapple food intake and began to properly nourish my body.

When being satanically abused, they attempt to misshape your body, mind, and psychological, emotional, energetic, and spiritual selves into opposite forms. For example, they will confuse the terms *love* and *hate* as well as *God* and *Satan*. The use of satanic language is common in satanic abuse, whereby they combine letters to create their own coded words. Some would say it has a sound similar to German, and I would agree with that comparison. As a child, you begin to become so heavily programmed that you are not sure what is real or unreal. However, at some inner level of mercy and grace, you know what is right and what is wrong.

As a child, I was told to do things that my slight girl body didn't want to do, and I knew it was not okay. Yet I was forced and threatened with my own death or the death of my pet dog and bird or my younger brothers if I said anything to anybody about the secrets. Adults had the control and power over me. These ritualistic abusive ceremonies happened weekly and oftentimes more frequently.

"I'm Tired"

(1995)

I just want to sleep.

Leave me alone.

I want my wrapped blankets

around me to keep you away,

to keep me warm and protected.

Leave me alone.

I need to sleep. I hear
you approaching.
Go away! Help me!
Where is my mother to comfort
and surround me with warmth
and protection?
Someone help!

There was truly nothing I could do to stop or escape their abuse. Often I was drugged or placed in a trance in order for the abusers to have complete control and the need to program or imprint core belief systems based on fear and hatred. The modus operandi, or goal, of satanic worship and abuse is to gather control of people and to spread this form of living: resentment, deceit, destruction, control, anxiety, pain, and hurt.

These untold and unspoken forms of programming I now readily expose. I thoroughly remember the details of the ceremonies, the specific words and tones of programming, places, times, music, and forms of symbols used. I also recall the types of drugs injected to gain access to your thoughts and several other pointed contents of their programs.

I have written a three hundred-page document that details every ceremony from birth of a female child until early adolescence. I believe these ceremonies that I expose will relate to the male children and how they were abused as well. Together we can journey where the path may lead us. I offer my hand and invite you to discover your own heart, one that is filled with love and peace. Collectively, we can make a difference. Quantum physics states, "The quiet flap of one soft butterfly wing influences Africa." This means that our intentions of peace really do affect a larger collective soul.

> *Pierce the veil of darkness and reveal its truth to light so that it pales into a faded background where sweet tones of music shine forth in gladness, with all hands, clasped in one circle of friendship.*
>
> —Doreen Virtue (author and speaker)

By exposing and talking freely, we are bringing this abuse to the light; therefore, it loses power. By exposing this form of abuse, it can no longer hide as a shadow after all. "Light does not cast the shadow; it reveals it." By continually exposing this abuse, we diminish it moment by moment until all that's left is your own Light.

> *Follow what lights you up and you'll Light Up the World. It doesn't matter how far our light shines, only that we shine it.*
>
> —Rebecca Campbell (author)

Now today after years of recovery, I truly believe we are all the manifestation of love. We are all born as love. That is who we are. However, as a child, adolescent, and young adult, up until my early thirties, I was living from fear.

As a child in school, I would rarely talk during large class discussion. Putting my hand up to answer questions or ask a question was rare. This was documented and reported from kindergarten through to the end of high school. It was also recorded early in my school years that I was having difficulty learning words and vowels and combinations of letters in order to create words. I was a severely shy one and was desperately sliding inside sadness and depression.

Eventually I numbed out completely and yet created a heightened sense of protection, naturally producing an acute sense of psychic self. This develops in children who are being abused because you need to be extraordinarily aware of every quiet sound, smell, and vision in order to draw in your protection of self.

When I was in high school, I wrote this poem about an artist. Somewhere inside of me, I had hope and a tiny light that shone and guided me as I really wanted to become an artist.

"The Artist"
(Written in Grade 11)
An artist or creator
takes simple life and
creates the flawless
images presented by
her talent.
She sits, draws, and creates images.
The plain scenery is
suddenly swirled into
a fantasy or myth of
the creator's imagination.

Dreaming is her life,

her wealth, and success.

A simple leaf is blown

into a colorful dancing fairy.

The white summer beach becomes

a hazy, pastel creation.

Winter snowfall is carved into a large diamond

as each sparkle becomes a snowflake.

The "nighttime sun" is romanced

into a sequin riding a

black, velvety blanket.

When the artist's dream is over,

her footsteps leave quietly,

carrying her packed dream

with her.

I learned at a very young age how to read people and yet trusted no one. I felt alone, and I believed I belonged to no one. Therefore I shut down my whole self, yet my sixth sensory system of protection was formed. It was all I had.

As stated earlier, I remember small pieces of my life outside of the abuse. Only through my recovery phase did I understand why I couldn't remember. When I do recall happy events, I recall with my heart and thankfulness. I remember taking piano lessons so that by the time I was in grade ten I had achieved my grade-eight piano certificate and music theory qualifications.

I loved music, dancing, and art. I do recall a foggy memory of me escaping into the fields and forest, all alone. We lived in the country just outside of the village, and in memory, I vaguely see myself running through a field to a tiny creek. Exploring nature was vital for me. The forest was my breath and sigh of release and safety. I was drawn to the rhythm of nature and would touch the dirt, trees, and rocks. I would feel at home.

This quote speaks to me as I remember the little creek flowing below my childhood house, rippling across the rolling fields. "The water doesn't concern itself with what rock it passes."

Still today as an adult, music, art, dance, and nature are a big part of my life. I hold the good and cherished memories tight with me forever. Here is a beautiful line that I found in my writings from one of my grade-eleven poems, which represented my need to be calm. "Kiss the relaxation of the silence as you sit and glisten at the velvet night."

" *Look deep into Nature, and then you will understand everything better.* "

—Albert Einstein (theoretical physicist)

As a child, I was often sick and in pain. This I remember and recollect so many bouts of colds, flu, bronchitis, bladder, yeast and kidney infections, fevers, mumps, and chicken pox. I had braces placed on my legs because I was told I would trip over my inward-turned feet. I have seen a photo of me with these metal braces and yet have no memory at all of this event.

As I travelled along my healing pathway, I would say to myself, "I am doing a great job," "I am love," "I am safe," "I am peace," and "I am okay." I would mantra this for me and about me, even when I didn't feel nor believe it to be true. When I went outside for my daily ten-kilometer run, I would literally say in every running step, "I am love." Often I was crying in my running steps because I couldn't feel this love inside of me . . . not yet. However, I knew the day would come when I would be able to feel this love and soft sensation, a day where I believed I was important, worthy, and loved, a day where I could begin a new and kinder life.

The part that wants to talk about it is your true self emerging. There is a hushed and vulnerable piece of my heart's tenderness that I would like to open up, share, and place easily upon these pages. I am patient in placing these words in sentence form. I am, as if, affectionately sinking into a stillness and in relation to my soul searching to find the words in order to honor another soul that was inside my sixteen-year-old body.

This experience taught me empathy, compassion, and, most of all, forgiveness. I write this with tears of healing falling from my eyes to your heart. If in any way you have had this following experience, please know that it was not your fault. Please know that the tiny baby's soul is now safely placed in the kind wings of angels forever. This I know for sure.

During the unspeakable abuse, I was forced to do acts that are now fully forgiven, and love streams through these acts. Through the encounters of abuse, I was continually raped by the group or one man while others were watching. In my heart and the abyssal center of my existence, I know that Little One, a baby sacrificed that was taken from me when I was a sixteen-year-old girl, is safely and tightly swaddled in the exquisite wings of the Angels of Love and Serenity. I know this to be true from the bottom of my ever so grasping core of my heart's existence as Spirit in human form. The pregnancy through rape is a complex part for me to speak about, and only I can feel and know the meaning in my heart of a sadness that still remains packaged in forgiveness.

I realize that those of us who encountered such trauma have hope and are truly boundlessly forgiven. We had no choice and were forced and strapped down to be part of this hideous abuse. A number of years ago, I had a quiet, cherished celebration for my baby, whom I will always name as "Little One."

At the base of an ancient local tree, I buried an elegant container filled with special items and gems and words of love in honor of Little One. At one point, I felt a gentle, warm feeling hug me around my shoulders as I stated my words dedicated to Little One. Tears flooded down my face as I knew that Little One was holding me and letting me know everything was okay now. This was still so hard for me. I needed strength.

This was a beloved tree to me and a wise friend. Still to this very day, it remains standing all alone in a large field—tall, strong, wise, and a bit bent over, neither weak nor broken.

Be still my heart,
these trees are prayers

—Rabindranath Tagore (Indian poet)

This meaningful celebration for me for a tiny being was beautiful and perplexing, all at the same time.

I prayed with forgiveness. I prayed with sadness. I prayed with guilt, shame, and blame. I prayed with all I had for the absolute forbearance of Little One's soul.

Even within the opening repair of my heart, there is not one singular day that slips by where I don't think of Little One.

If this experience were part of your own background, I say to you from the divinity of my heart, "You are forgiven. Feel all of the feelings of guilt, shame, and fear, and loosen them gently, slowly, and carefully. Their little souls, I promise you, are being taken care of within the purity of love."

My intense therapy and deprogramming treatment concluded around 2008, after approximately fifteen years of therapy, once or twice a week. Making the decision to release and shift through this was the best decision of my life. This included a variety of treatments from psychotherapy to a deprogramming specialist, a psychologist, life coach, Reiki energy master, homeopathic doctor, emotion therapist specialist, osteopathic doctor, spiritual advisor, crystal healer, sacral/cranial specialist, attachment-releasing therapist, sound therapy, restorative yoga, deep tissue massage, body memory releasing, tapping, Shaman past-life discovery, and more. I was not giving up!

I released or deprogrammed hundreds of satanic programs and attachments. As this was processing through me, I was feeling sick and crazy. Yet what happened to me was crazy! Essentially what can happen is that people won't believe you, which then makes you doubt yourself or even confirm that perhaps you are crazy. You begin to doubt yourself. However, what happened was crazy, and it wasn't me. Not a lot has been written about this form of abuse due to its complexity and layered pieces.

A number of years ago, I attended a conference where Dr. Barbara DeAngelis was speaking. Not only is she a speaker, she is an author and media personality, She was one of the leaders in developing the self-help movement in the 1980s. Her book, *Soul Shifts* (Hay House 2015), is a practical guide to higher awareness. I believe she is able to look at shadows and see the light caught within.

After her amazing talk, I decided to stand in an hourlong line to meet her and share my childhood story as well as have her sign her published book for me.

As I was delicately sharing parts of my childhood story, she moved in close to me with compassionate eyes. Then at that moment, I knew she was a vehicle for a message for me. She said, "Make it not your story. Go past the story. Go to the deeper level, that soul level. Where from here, then you can move forward."

This was one of the most incredible statements anyone has ever suggested to me about my childhood. I didn't know what to say to her but "thank you." Her statement changed everything for me. Life is really only about love! At a deeper soul level, there is a profound forgiveness and a love so pure that it feels like a wonderful, warm liquid that is indescribable. There are no words.

These pages I write in pursuit that, if only one person were helped along his or her journey, then my soul will fill with a transcendent love. I will then ask you, "How can I assist? Be strong and brave, and hold hope tightly within your entire being."

I often would listen to the song "Instrument of Peace" by Olivia Newton-John, a gorgeous rendition of the St. Francis of Assisi Prayer. This song always illuminates my life and helps me move into my day.

"Instrument of Peace"

Olivia Newton-John, *Grace and Gratitude* (2006)

Where there is hatred, let me bring love.

Where there is doubt, let me bring faith.

Where there is falsehood, let me bring truth.

Where there is pain, I'll comfort you.

Where there is silence, let me sing praise.

Where there's despair, let me bring hope.

Where there is blindness, let me bring sight.

Where there is darkness, let me bring light.

Elie Wiesel (1928–2016) was fifteen years old when he was deported to Auschwitz. He lived through deplorable torture that he calls "events." He became a journalist and writer after the war, and he wrote over fifty books, including his masterwork, *Night*, a major best-seller revealing the "events." He was awarded several medals of honor, and in 1986, he was the recipient of the Nobel Peace Prize. I discovered his book, *Open Heart* (Schocken 2012), and I am honored to quote and paraphrase Wiesel here in the pages of my book.

He was a phenomenal man, survivor, and soul. His use of words in his writings has been best described as "quiet dialogue" and "eloquent and poignant clarity." Wiesel stated, "For my conscience—thus my being—continues to carry hope." He was convinced that, no matter what happens in life, there is light, love, and hope.

"I continue to cling to words because it is up to us to transform them into instruments of comprehension, rather than those of contempt. It is up to us to choose whether we wish to use them to curse or to heal, to wound or to console."

As I continue to write and position my words to communicate to you, the reader, my time of darkness, followed by hope, every word, sentence, and paragraph emulates an experience that defies all comprehension. However, stay with the words, and you will witness the transformation. And you may gather a very personal message that is directed to you.

I am writing this portion of this book, which was still in manuscript form, on New Year's Eve. I just learned that tomorrow, which is January 1, is a full moon. The full moon on New Year's Day is so powerful as it gives us a push to rid us of onerous habits, old patterns, thoughts, and behaviors. I wish to share with you this definition:

> " *The full moon's energy teaches us about being true to yourself and how to parent yourself. This moon governs our childhood, upbringing, our relationship to our parents or parental figures, and the ways we developed emotionally in the world; therefore, a full moon and especially in a New Year is the perfect time to consider these things.* "

—Rosey Baker

In other words, working with the power of the full moon will amp up the intention to resolve, release, and clear. How perfectly timed this is in order to pull the exquisite healing power of the full moon upon these pages in a grace-filled manner.

> " *Weeping may endure for a night, but joy comes in the morning.* "

—Anonymous

During my recovery work, I noticed that, as one program or memory was deprogrammed or released, I started to feel much better—lighter, more open, and able to breathe. I was feeling a sprinkle of hope dusting through me that was indescribable to me at that time. I was convinced even further that I must continue into the depths of this darkness in order to break free.

Even when I felt a stream of light and sunshine on my face, I knew then it was time for the greatest sojourn of my life. Yes, it is unfathomable the amount of pain you feel as you release. The rage of my bleeding wounds surfaced and threw me to the ground in unabashed humility and vulnerability.

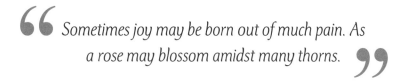

Sometimes joy may be born out of much pain. As a rose may blossom amidst many thorns.

—Anonymous

I was being stripped away, and the cocoon was coming off me. The flashbacks poured out of me, followed by even more. Perhaps you can't even imagine the memories unless you've been there yourself. This was the toughest work I had ever endured and yet the most important and inspiring. I sought to be unbound and liberated, to live a cherished joyful life enveloped with kindness. I do understand and stand not before you or ahead of you, but with you to say, "It's all okay for you. You can do this!"

I am not special. I just decided one day that I wanted to see and feel the light. I discovered that the present was worth living, and to loosen the past now was imperative. I refused to give in!

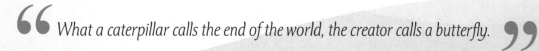

What a caterpillar calls the end of the world, the creator calls a butterfly.

—Richard Bach (author)

If you are a therapist and have been hearing some pieces of disjointed memories of satanic abuse, I encourage you to allow your client to first and foremost feel safe as well as be believed, listened to, understood, and loved.

When I started therapy, I was numb and dissociative and candidly couldn't feel feelings at all, let alone love for anyone or myself. My voyage entailed learning how to socialize and be present without dissociating. One of my amazing therapists gave me an intellectual descriptive listing of one hundred feelings we display. I felt only "blank, devoid of any feelings." I had to first intellectually understand emotions.

There were also many moments of when during a conversation I actually wouldn't remember what the other person just communicated to me. Their language and my comprehension of what this person stated to me went, once again, "blank." I would then not be able to respond inside the conversation because I had no words and I couldn't hear the other person. Their lips were moving, but I didn't understand their language.

At that time, some professionals labelled this as an auditory process learning disability. That wasn't the case. It was a trigger to certain words, and in the trigger of the words, I dissociated or numbed out. When numbing out in conversation, you actually don't hear the words. It will present itself as a learning disability. I was triggered by many words, and when those words were verbally stated and, in some cases, combined, I would numb out subconsciously.

Yet I would consciously be very aware of the blanking out of conversation. Often I would just not engage in any social conversation because I couldn't follow the conversation. I would remain silent. It wasn't until I discovered that some of the words that people stated generated a trigger response. The person would have no idea that I was triggered, and some people would even say to me, "Sarah, you just asked me this same question, and I already answered." I needed to pursue the releasing and deprogramming of certain words in order to set me free to be social.

As a result, I didn't have the basic social skills developed due to the abuse or trauma. The parental teachings were absent of any form of socialization. If our family visited others, I would remain mute, and my mother would speak for me. My voice left me. This developed into a co-dependent relationship with my mother, who made all of my life's decisions since I had no feelings or understanding of even how to complete the act of making decisions. This included what to wear, who to date, what to eat, and who to be friends with. One of the first steps of my recovery was to heal the co-dependency I had with my mother.

If you are a survivor of any form of abuse, allow yourself to persevere and move through it. What you have gone through could make you be the one who can teach the "through" and help others, if that is your calling. I discovered that, with each memory release, your truth bursts through an opening, and this opening is classified as the revealing of your authentic self.

Furthermore in the depths of releasing memories, my feelings finally began to move and strive forward. I felt as though I would lose control of dealing with the fear of feeling everything to the extreme. However, my feelings surfaced, and I began to love myself a bit more each day and became aware of the safety in flushing out my feelings.

Satanic abuse internalizes the ritualistic ceremonies that programmed me to believe I was weak, not loved, not loveable, not worth anything, and fearful. I believed nobody cared about me, and I created a perception of the world that I truly was alone.

In some tribal practices, the tribe wounds you so profoundly that you will return back to them, which is exactly how satanic cult activity develops. They attempt to program you to live in fear and anger, and you have a need for revenge and living your life with deep sadness.

If you are living this way and this is your background, it may mean you are still living and believing their base belief system. This can now become your choice! Don't let fear be your choice. The wound is the place where light enters you.

The more you live in fear, the more fear you create, and it is mirrored and attracted back to you. This is the basic, mystical Law of Attraction, an energy-based system whereby it states, "What you focus upon most is what will be attracted back to you." It also means, if you will it, it will happen.

> " *The more you see yourself as what you'd like to become, and act as if what you want is already there, the more you'll activate those dormant forces that will collaborate to transform your dream into your reality.* "

—Wayne Dyer (spiritual teacher, author, and speaker)

Feelings are magnetic.
Each feeling is a beacon that attracts a reality.
Love attracts love.
Generosity elicits a generous response.
Anger creates more things that could make
you even angrier—if you let them.
What we focus on expands.
So choosing to focus on life-affirming feelings is the
surest way to create the experience you want.
—Danielle Laporte

If your thoughts, emotions, behaviors, and energy output are all based on fear, then you will receive all this fear mirrored back to you. This is what satanic programming is all about.

I finally realized this and woke up! If I continued to live from feeling betrayed, fearful, and angry, then I am still living under their abusive rulings. They attempt to wound you in fear in order to pull you back to their teachings. Why would I want to live the rest of my life in fear? No more! I want to live from love. I believe we are all wired to live extraordinary lives.

> " *She left the old story behind her and stepped into a new once upon a time.* "
>
> —Rebecca Campbell (speaker, author, and teacher)

I once heard that we don't live "on" the planet but "in" the planet between an illusion that reflects or manifests ego-based beliefs and without an illusion where there is only a loving, kind, Spirit Essence. Both of these perceptions are real, according to the one you may base your life on or the one you believe in.

Our Planet Earth isn't solely a slab of rock. It is a living being or organism that breathes with a heartbeat and rhythm streaming with emotions. The way in which you live your life determines the Earth's existence and how we situate our lives inside the Earth's heartbeat.

> " *If what I say resonates with you, it is merely because we are both branches of the same tree.* "
>
> —W. B. Yeats (poet)

I am going to tell you an old Cherokee Native story that I once heard told during a storytelling session. I listened in amazement as it further illuminated my heart to even deeper awakenings. My wish for you is that you will find it just as alluring.

This ancient story begins with an elder Cherokee grandfather speaking with his grandson about a battle that is going on inside of everyone. The elder remained still and silent in his facial expression as he began to slowly prepare and ever so delicately reveal one word followed by the next.

He looked softly into the eyes of his grandson, which allowed the child to settle and open his heart. The child then realized at some inner level of his soul that what he was about to hear would be life changing and he too one day would pass these teachings along to his own grandchildren.

The velvet, nighttime sky was calm, and the fire was burning low and quiet. The child looked up into the sky to honor the stars and moon and knew he would always remember this "moment of teaching from his grandfather."

He could sense a cool, effortless breeze shift through his body, and he understood that Nature and Spirit were ignited and ready to pass along the grand teaching from his grandfather. He was ready to receive. It was time.

The old Cherokee first placed his hands on his own heart and closed his eyes. This was a story about living from the heart. The elder began to ease the words into the story, "This is a story about two wolves. A battle is going on inside all of us. It is a terrible fight, and it is between these two wolves."

The child's eyes grew large with intrigue as he was once taught that the wolf's Spirit means being wise, feeling your intuition, and living from your true expression of self and freedom.

The grandfather spoke, "One wolf is consumed with anger. He is layered with envy, greed, lies, self-pity, arrogance, inferiority, and ego. The other wolf is consumed with peace, kindness, empathy, truth, and compassion and radiates joy."

The grandson sat very still for a moment, as if frozen inside the story that would soon shine forth in providing its life lesson. He glanced toward the sky and then looked intensely inside his grandfather's eyes and asked, "Which wolf will win the fight, Grandfather?"

The old Cherokee spoke with a voice of Earthen wisdom as he knew at this very moment this was the lesson for his grandson. He simply replied, "The one you feed, Grandchild."

The grandson felt this lesson shape his heart. A tingly sensation surged through his body, and the story's imprint laid its lesson.

Today that grandson is now a grandfather and is preparing to relay this message to his own grandchild. This story changed his view on life and his life choices.

This "Story of Two Wolves" speaks of the teaching from an old Cherokee to his grandson on how to carry his life from the choices he makes. This story is the connecting fiber to our movement toward living from kindness, caring, and just a softness. Conceiving a reality feeding from this positive energy or feelings will just attract more of the same and even beyond. This generates an ongoing replenishment of positive feelings of going beyond negative thought patterns and behaviors. When you shift away from happiness, you are really shifting away from yourself.

 It's often best to do the opposite of what your fear is telling you to do.

—Danielle Laporte (author and inspirational speaker)

Another great author I found is Eldon Taylor, psychotherapist, speaker, teacher, and author who wrote *Mind Programming* (Hay House 2009). Taylor explores the fundamentals or keys to living a brilliant life and reaching far inside oneself to capture the power within in order to move forward. He states, "I believe in the human potential and its evolution toward love and peace. I believe in you … When each of us awakens to our individual potential, we lead the way to a conscious awakening of the planet as a whole."

Taylor believes that the most powerful force in the world is love. "It cancels fear, which is the only obstacle to overcome so that all of our experiences can take on new dimensions of meaning and joy."

How would you answer these statements?

If I weren't afraid, I would …

What would you do if you weren't afraid of making a mistake, feeling rejected, or being alone? Would you love more deeply, wear purple pants, and be your true self?

I love myself so much that …

Would you eat healthy foods, sleep more, spend time alone, or even leave a relationship?

" *It doesn't interest me where or what or with whom you have studied. I want to know what sustains you, from the inside, when all else falls away.* "

—Oriah Mountain Dreamer (author and poet)

I decided it was time for me to set goals for each day. I ask myself, "What is the most important thing for me to focus upon today?" Then I give gratitude at the end of every day. I decided it was time to stop minimizing myself day after day. It was time to love me and allow myself to be loved by others. I needed to feel love through and then beyond my wounds.

 This is my wonderful day. I have never seen this one before.

—Maya Angelou (author, poet, and playwright)

My journal entries started to reshape themselves with an exuberance and enthusiasm for life. A fortitude of promising tranquility and harmony began to fill my journal papers. My words slid from despair to tackling despair. I was now not wishing for hope, but "living in hope" and "living in love." My journals shaped themselves into dream books.

"A Place" (2011)
I am relaxed and have arrived in a place
that creates the love and passion for life.
I remember that, as I create my world, I also create
all that is around me in every area in my life.
Be still inside,
allowing myself to be peaceful and full of peace.
Be joyful and joy-filled—loving and kind.
I now allow kindness to rule my day
and allow the way of life for me to be the one I am,
which means I am then allowing myself the dignity
to just simply be love and only love and nothing more.

I was intuitively creating art as well as writings during my healing process. I loved drawing and painting still life, which are simple collections of fruit, jars, and vases with flowers, as taught by my grandmother. One piece in particular I created using pencil crayons, skinny charcoal, pastels, and thin markers. It was a still life sketch of a banana, apple, and clear glass vase with a single flower elegantly displayed through the glass.

After the drawing was complete, I took a pair of scissors and cut the picture up. Then I carefully placed it back together, much like a puzzle, as I attached the pieces. However, I left spaces between the pieces and wrote these words in between the pieces. The title of my artwork is "The Still of Life Is Broken."

"The Still of Life Is Broken" (1995)

Everything is broken; nothing fits.

I'm broken; I'm broken.

Where is my life?

I can't find my whole self.

I'm broken, broken.

Nothing fits! Help me!

Fragmented … fragmented.

Help me!

I'm broken inside, upside down

and all in pieces.

Somebody help me!

What inevitably started to reshape in my life were not only my poems but my art. I released my sadness and pain through poetry and art in order to step inside a new form of poetry, one filled with hope and promise. As a result, my art in turn began to attentively turn into huge collage pieces of texture, and I would implement a variety of media to convey calmness, glamour, and joy. My artwork transitioned from dark to absolutely beautiful.

> *I want to know if you can be with joy, mine or your own, if you can dance with wildness and let the ecstasy fill you to the tips of your fingers and toes without cautioning us to be careful, to be realistic.*
>
> —Oriah Mountain Dreamer (author and poet)

I encourage everyone who is treading through any form of healing to find a release point. Mine was art and writing poetry. As I searched through old boxes stacked with poems, journals, and art, I discovered I was ready to share my art and poetry throughout the pages of this book.

I was learning not to dwell so much on the challenges I was facing. I now understood that the subconscious mind, by its very nature, accepts all of my feelings associated with troubles, actually as a request. Then it continues to make them my experiences in the world. It is our divine right and choice to feel great. This is our power of creation that we can live by on a daily basis.

> *Today is the First Day of the Rest of Your Life.*
>
> —American proverb

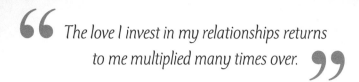

> *The love I invest in my relationships returns to me multiplied many times over.*
>
> —Alan Cohen (author and life coach)

I remember hearing this quote somewhere, "The chance to love and be loved exists no matter where you are." I realized I was rebirthing my true self, which was only of love and peace. I started to trust a bit more, and then happiness started to really blossom forth for me. An excitement to live life was available for me, and I was feeling joy for the first time in my life. Joy is not a thing or an item. It is in us.

Trusting was a big one for me. I needed to be taught how to trust. The skill base or the foundation of not only not trusting myself but everybody around me wasn't built inside of me, and the relearning was painful, however necessary. I learned very quickly that I was a controlling person, and I actually didn't realize this about myself. It was a natural instinct that developed inside of me to keep me safe. When one is controlling, you are trying to not feel pain and are afraid of losing control.

This situation for me would mean I was being too vulnerable, emotional, and open. Inevitably this would create pain. At least this was my belief that I was taught to believe, which was as an end product of the abuse. So now I was learning about how to be vulnerable and open and knowing that I am safe.

> *If you peel back the layers of your life—the frenzy, the noise—stillness is waiting. That stillness is you.*
>
> —Oprah

Victor E. Frankl was an internationally renowned psychiatrist who endured years of unspeakable horror in Nazi death camps. He wrote *Man's Search for Meaning*, and it was first published in 1946. Over three million copies sold and continue to sell. While living inside the concentration camp, he came to a conclusion. "A thought transfixed me: for the first time in my life I saw the truth as it is set into song by so many poets, proclaimed as the final wisdom by so many thinkers. The truth—that love is the ultimate and the highest goal of which man can aspire."

Even in his darkness, he awakened to his truth of knowing and feeling that he is just love. I feel that, when you live inside a dark place, there comes a point when you do see a light, even if it is small and just a slight glimmer. Deep inside all of us, we truly know there is a light. We really do! It is that unexplained part of you that eventually encourages you to get out of bed or says to you, "Don't say that to your friend, or you will destroy this friendship." It is that true loving self that is and what is continually offering us guidance.

Perhaps we genuinely do learn from our stillness. When we listen and nimbly motion into this stillness, we find ourselves.

I remember when healing through the flashbacks that a memory emerged of when I was six years old. I saw a large golden angel walking beside me during one of the ritualistic, abusive ceremonies. She said to me, "Dear Sweet One, you will be okay, and I am here with you always."

This image I can still clearly see and feel today. The warmth of this angel kept me calm and hopeful that someone was with me and loved me. I learned later that this golden angel was my Guardian Angel. No matter what, hope, love, and peace will make itself known to you—no matter what.

"Work like you don't need the money. Love like nobody has ever hurt you. Dance like nobody is watching. Sing like nobody is listening. Live as if this was paradise on Earth."

Anonymous

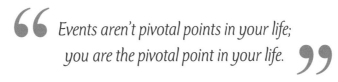

Events aren't pivotal points in your life;
you are the pivotal point in your life.

—Eldon Taylor (author and inventor)

Reach for that sacred space inside of you, that sparkle, that Light, that original Spirit, that Source, that love deep within you. Whatever term you choose to use, it is that part of who you really are and can never ever be destroyed. They could never take or destroy that part of me ... ever. No matter what type of abuse.

In *A Course in Miracles*, the author Helen Schucman states, "Nothing real can be threatened. Nothing unreal exists."

Marianne Williamson, spiritual teacher, author, and lecturer, speaks clearly about love and the illusion of fear. "Love is the all-encompassing reality and thus can have no opposite. Love is the only eternal truth, while fear is the hallucination of the mortal mind. Fear-mind is referred to as ego. Illusions can not stand in the presence of love."

This doesn't mean we look away or deny the horrible acts of abuse and pretend it doesn't exist. But rather, look through them, thus gesturing in a world that lies beyond. It's more about realizing that illusions, no matter how entrenched they might be within the three-dimensional world, cannot stand in the presence of love.

> " *The body is not eternal, but the soul is. Such is the miracle:*
> *A tale about despair becomes a tale against despair.* "
>
> —Elie Wiesel (writer, professor, and Holocaust survivor)

I have come to a conclusion that, inside my life, everything was transformed for me. I believe that I chose this route to experience satanic abuse in order to make a complete U-turn and to pop out into the light. I should probably no longer say I am a survivor of satanic abuse. I am not identified as this!

Instead I will say, "I have experienced satanic abuse and survived to speak about this unspeakable abuse." I could have held onto it and created more fear and ignored it, but I released it. I don't want to be identified by it. This was a journey I went through in order to soar as high and as far as I can in love. It happened not "to" me, but "for" me. However, sometimes I feel that those who have been hurt the most have the greatest ability to help heal others.

> " *Energy flows where your attention goes. Just as the flower*
> *opens up to the light, your soul opens up to self love.* "
>
> —Lao Tzu (philosopher and writer)

After residing in such a dark place and living so low, I decided to turn this childhood background into a calling of beauty, love, purpose, and courage. This abuse has set me on a path to help others as an Intuitive Counsellor, motivational public speaker, author, teacher, and artist.

I do valiantly feel that it will be those of us who survived this abuse who should expose it. It will be up to us to do something positive. Collectively we remain strong in our hearts and within our love of life! As survivors of this type of abuse, we are unique and amazing. We know things and have seen the darkness. We are empowered, powerful, and just often happy to be alive, and we have learned to cherish every single moment of each day.

> *We must be the change we wish to see in the world.*
>
> —Mahatma Gandhi

> I now say:
> I am love,
> I am peace,
> I am joy,
> I am happy,
> I am free.
> What energy opens a rose
> you can't destroy it,
> It does nothing and
> leaves nothing undone.
>
> —Anonymous

Even if you are unable to feel this love inside of you, don't worry. It is there. We are all born as love. The satanic programs attempt to convince you to believe the illusion that you are not love. A good friend of mine once said to me, "We are the manifestation of love, and anything outside of love is an illusion."

When I was stepping gingerly into deeper forms of recovery, for many years, I started to feel resentment, anger, blame, rage, and betrayal to those who hurt me over and over again. Eventually this heaviness evaporated away, but it was vital to feel and then gently, yet strongly, be released. I was beginning to ask myself, "What brings me joy?" I wanted to live beyond ordinary parts of the universe. I remember being moved when hearing a version of the song, "I Can See Clearly Now," sung by Holly Cole. As I listened, I felt filled with these shivers of finally knowing that "I can see clearly now."

"I Can See Clearly Now"

I can see clearly now,

The rain is gone,

I can see all obstacles in my way.

Gone are the dark clouds that had me blind,

It's gonna be a bright, sunshiny day.

I think I can make it now.

All of the bad feelings have disappeared.

There is the rainbow I've been praying for.

Holly Cole, *Don't Smoke in Bed* (1993)

There flourished a point in time when a different understanding flooded my heart and an awakening broke through. I endeavored to walk upon the road to forgiveness to those who hurt me. I call it "giving forth love" because these people are also heavily programmed, injured, wounded, and lost in this dark way of living. They are scared and scarred.

When I authentically and honestly felt this in my heart and in prayer, I then travelled to visit my parents and forgave them. This does not mean that what happened was right … because it was not. I just accepted, cleared, cleaned, and shifted forward, and for me personally, I needed to hug them and bring peace, a closure. I then decided to break away from my family. The feelings of mourning and grieving about my family indisputably will at times rise up and flood through me. However, many years now have slid by, and I continue to send my prayers and blessings to my family.

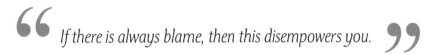

> *If there is always blame, then this disempowers you.*
>
> —Anonymous

They remain trapped inside the programs with a clarity of life that is skewed and uncertain. By stepping into forgiveness and light, I felt a further and immense sense of freedom. Something had released in this true forgiveness while I was giving my parents love. I truly believe that my healing has also helped my family in an energetic way. I decided that, instead of blame, I take responsibility for my own healing.

> *As long as we blame, we effectively eliminate our ability to grow, to be in control, or to experience peace, balance, and harmony. The power to grow resides in forgiveness. Letting go will set us free. Forgiving everyone, including ourselves, provides the opportunity to become more than we have been.*
>
> —Eldon Taylor (author and inventor)

Let it be known that the truth is within each of us. It is here and always has been. It has never left. Do not worry or fret. The truth is you and only you. You are the keeper of the truth.

Many of the other satanic members who abused me may still be alive, and I only send love and prayers to their hearts. Maybe one day an awakening for them will happen, and then they too will live in freedom.

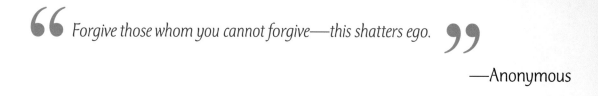

Forgive those whom you cannot forgive—this shatters ego.

—Anonymous

In the releasing process, there truly is a "real-ease," which is your freedom, your authentic self, and your sacred place. Everyone is able to claim their true self.

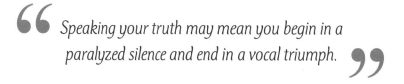

Speaking your truth may mean you begin in a paralyzed silence and end in a vocal triumph.

—Anonymous

I believe that life is about experiencing the experience and what you can do with this experience in a positive way. It's about how you approach the experience. It is amazing how a crisis or trauma can be morphed into a profound transformation and can change your life forever in a very gracious way.

Every day I give gratitude for the life I am enjoying now. I have rewritten my destiny. I sensed that, when my soul received a glimpse of my truth, I could never go back. Moving forward and more deeply inside of my heart was my only option. I truly believe that I have been the beneficiary or inheritor of so many miracles in my life.

One miracle that saved and redesigned my life happened on my thirty-seventh birthday. I was in the midst of the darkness of my recovery work when everything exhausted me: to breathe, to open my eyes, to eat, and even to walk. I was encountering unbearable memories that included the inability to think straight as well as evolving and revolving emotions, with triggers surfacing more often. I was inside the depths of despair and felt too tired. I just wanted to just sleep forever.

I was writing in my journal on the evening of my thirty-seventh birthday that I was done and needed to give in to fatigue. I couldn't do this! This was becoming too difficult. I thought, *I can't have another memory of hurt and pain. I am so shaken and fragile. I just can't go on.*

At the exact moment, I decided I was too tired and wanted to stop my recovery work. Suddenly a warmth expanded from inside of me and near me. It was instantaneous, and an immediate deep awakening happened. The feeling was surreal, and one of pure love and calmness overtook me spontaneously and completely. I continued to write in my journal but without effort or thinking. The words or messages fell from my pen onto the paper as if someone else were controlling my hand. A soft, velvet, yet imperative voice was penetrating my own thoughts and existence.

The feelings and words were peaceful, joyful with a knowing that I was a vessel for the messages of beauty to move through me from a loving, Godly Spirit. Devoted, divine care pulled me from the edge. That took place over fifteen years ago, and since that time, I have created more than thousands of handwritten pages, all compiled to create published books, a series of healing cards, plus a curriculum for self-development. My life instantly changed.

The question I now ask, "Is it possible to arrive so close to the edge without something miraculous changing and shifting inside of us?"

I now know that what I encountered in my childhood landscape that, if it didn't change my life, then I wasn't paying attention to my heart. However, I did pay attention and found me. I found life and breath.

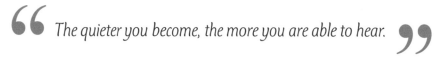

The quieter you become, the more you are able to hear.

—Rumi (poet and theologian)

Do not wait until tomorrow. Say, do, or make it happen now. Go where you need to be. Do not wait to be invited to places. Host your own parties. Do not sit by the phone. Pick it up. Spread the word. Press the buttons. Buy the tickets and enjoy the show.

> *Just be in a state of gratitude. What you risk reveals what you value.*
>
> —Jeanette Winterson (novelist)

In writing this book, I feel it was part of my destiny or calling. Yes, it took years before I wrote it, but a button was pushed in my heart when I saw the deep sadness and hurt inside the eyes of one of my kindergarten students.

As an elementary schoolteacher, my heart is filled with a sense of love and passion for teaching children. But these tiny eyes of one of my students called out to my personal heart and hurt. I felt alone as a child, but now I can be there for some hurts I can see in children. So this book was written within weeks of seeing this wee child's eyes and sensing their pain and loneliness. I needed to get out of my way, out of my own fears, and step up. Otherwise, it hurts too much for what I know and not to do anything about it. This isn't about me, but how I am now being called to help.

> *The things I do—I do because it hurts not to. Things revealed to us, the ugliness we know. But we know this ugliness because we have to do something about it.*
>
> —Sherlock Holmes

When I allowed myself to sink into therapy, there was a point when I remembered being a grade-five student. I was sitting in my regular class, and the special education teacher came into our class and called out the names of the students with special needs (students diagnosed with developmental disabilities, learning difficulties, and emotional challenges). They would always line up at the door and walk down to the special education room for their modified work time.

But this time my own name was called. This had never happened before. I remember leaving the classroom with these children and feeling my heart falling into my stomach. I sat on a chair in the small room and watched the two special education teachers look at me from the doorway and quietly talk to each other.

I remember thinking, *They know something*. Then they asked me to go back to my classroom. Neither of them said anything to me. Today that one singular memory of grade five further confirmed for me that something was askew in my little girl life.

Perhaps I had bruises, looked extremely tired, was sick, or showed other signs of abuse. This was during the early 1970s when childhood abuse wasn't spoken about or addressed. This memory of these two teachers looking with concern at me and talking at the entry of the special education room's door still remains encapsulated as a confirmation for me that something was wrong in my childhood. The teachers just couldn't say anything, unless they actually did? I may never know.

Today as a special education and kindergarten teacher, I ensure that I imprint love to all of my students. I tell them I believe in them and try my very best to create amazing memories and to reinforce that they are worthy, wonderful, and fantastic children. Maybe one day they will need to draw up that memory to help them along their journey. I wish to gift them courage because one person believed in them.

> *" We are all being called to action, not from an angry heart, but from a heart so filled with love that it melts the darkness within those who would hurt the children. "*

—Doreen Virtue (author and speaker)

I say "thank you" to these two special education teachers who helped me because this miraculous memory was an opened window, and as a result, it kept me advancing forward through therapy. Something was noticed about me then, and this memory of so few memories of childhood was imprinted to help me heal.

This memory is now over forty years ago. As teachers today, we can now call agencies even if we have a suspicion of abuse. We are taught to look for the signs and symptoms. I know, feel, and sense when a child has been or is being abused. This is not uncommon when you come from this background. You just *know*. Other survivors will say the same thing. It is a look in the child's eyes or an energy you feel.

We all need to be kind and not get so caught up in a sequenced, intellectual-based, educational curriculum, but to come from an emotional and living curriculum whereby children are able to feel safe, develop emotions, and learn to interact with social functional skills. My next project is to write children's books for specific purposes of assisting in their authentic development and discovering their true hearts.

Although I often feel that children are the teachers, not the adults. They can teach us how to be present in the moment and how easily it is to watch a ladybug for hours. We all need to cultivate inspiration, laughter, surprise, simplicity, and curiosity.

Never withhold praise. I read somewhere, "One of the greatest offerings we can give another person is to truly witness their gifts." When we witness the gifts of another, we are actually witnessing their soul and light within them.

Let's just be kind and help each other. What would happen if we taught our children early in life that the world is a safe place and that love is everywhere and everyone is kind? This change we wish to see must first start in us. We must now be that change. The change is actually a transformational state of consciousness.

It's time to turn on a brand-new light.

When I have publicly spoken about my journey at conferences or to smaller groups, I play the song "Believe In You" by Amanda Marshall. The words speak about believing in yourself and a person reciprocating love by believing in you.

"Believe In You"

Somewhere there's a river, looking for a stream.

Somewhere there's a dreamer, looking for a dream.

Somewhere there's a drifter, trying to find his way.

I will hold you up, I will comfort you.

Somewhere someone's waiting to hear

"I believe in you."

I can't even count the ways I believe in you.

All I want to do is to help you believe in you.

Amanda Marshall, *Tuesday's Child* (1999)

I do feel that, when I started to believe and trust in my heart and give myself intuitive hugs, then life opened up.

 You are built not to shrink down to less, but to blossom into more. To be more splendid. To use every moment to fill yourself up.

—Oprah

You can't hide a light. Eventually everything became clearer for me. As I let go of negative traits and belief systems, I discovered my true nature. *Change Your Thoughts, Change Your Life* (Hay House 2007) by Wayne Dyer, teacher, speaker, and author, spoke to me during my recovery.

He talked about how everything remains the same until a change happens, which means that nothing happens until something moves. If you can't imagine yourself differently, then you will stay the same. He surmised, "New thoughts lead to new experiences. New experiences lead to new thoughts." Therefore, the same choices from the same thoughts create the same experience. The way you think, react, and feel creates your personality or your "person-reality."

 There is one grand lie—that we are limited. The only limits we have are the limits we believe.

—Dr. Wayne W. Dyer (spiritual teacher, author, and speaker)

In 1903, James Allen wrote a literal essay entitled "As A Man Thinketh" (Filiquarian Publishing). It developed into one of the world's greatest self-help books. He wrote in substantial detail how our thoughts create our reality. "We are designed and built by our own thoughts in our mind. If we nurture negative thoughts, pain will soon follow. If our thoughts are healthy and beneficial, joy will follow us."

I just felt I had to write this again, "Joy started to burst out of me!" I am feeling happy and free. I am alive!

The space between our lives is where hope exists. The spaces were empty because the "goop" or the heavy energy of satanic programs was leaving me, and I knew and could feel there was hope. I decided it was time to live, with no time to waste. I wanted extraordinary love, which in Italian is the word amore. I found this quote from someplace, and I adore it. "When you take off your armor, you then find and experience amore."

The armor of protection is for safety and the armor of mistrust and not wanting to get hurt anymore or again. However, the journey is to be open, free, vulnerable, trusting, and real. I feel I have stopped the circulation of being stuck and rotating in the same muck with the same story. A friend of mine practices the Buddhist teachings, and one teaching is, "You can talk about your crisis or challenge three times then you must do something about it—just don't get caught in it." Don't stare! Just look at the past.

There is a great book by Ralph Waldo Trine, *In Tune With The Infinite* (Penguin 1897), which industrialists embraced. Henry Ford gave away hundreds of copies to colleagues, schoolteachers, laborers, homemakers, and students. Trine was a journalist and considered a motivational writer. Here is one of his great quotes.

Truth is within ourselves; it

takes no rise.

From outward things, whate'er you

may believe,

There is an inmost centre in us all,

Where truth abides in fullness.

Within yourself lies the cause

of whatever enters into your life.

To come into the full realization of

your own awakened interior

powers, is to be able

to condition your life in

exact accord with what

you would have it.

Trine writes about living your full potential and in an awakened state of heart. I love Oprah's quote, "How much farther can I stretch to reach my full potential?" I feel alive. I am alive, and I daily ask myself, "What's next? How can I make this very day amazing and extraordinary?"

" *One of the secrets of a happy life is continuous small treats.* "

—Iris Murdoch (novelist)

Today I love to write, create projects, and talk about new ideas and philosophical anthems in life. I love teaching younger children how to tap into their authentic selves. After teaching school during the day, I then participate in the next part of my day, which is my Intuitive Counselling or clairvoyant private practice. I have built a practice around my developed sixth sense. I help others to love and care for themselves. My passion is teaching individuals and groups of adults how to tap into their psychic/intuitive self, which is a blessing for me. Teaching meditation and being a founder of a healing center still warms my heart. I have met some of the most amazing, strong people, and I am gifted to be in their presence. Motivational public speaking sparkles in my heart! I am excited about my life.

Of course I do continue to walk upon my path of healing. Sometimes a boulder crosses my path, and I become bruised by bumping into it. However, I am learning to see better and understand more.

I do now welcome any form of challenge, whether that be emotional, psychological, mindful, or physical. I believe that, when moving through healing abuse, you definitely become stronger in all aspects of life. I am not an angry stronger, but a trusting stronger, loving individual. Through physically working out with personal trainers, I discovered I love physical exercise and seeing how far I can push my body. Through sessions of burpees, jumping jacks, push-ups, free weights, running obstacles, and more, all helped me immensely clear and release anxiety.

For a year, twice a week, one of my personal trainers, a retired boxer, taught me how to box. At first putting on the boxing wraps and gloves was daunting. She encouraged me to punch at the large, flat gloves she had in front of her face and body. I could hardly punch and felt after all that the anger had left me through fifteen years of intense therapy. Yet what I didn't realize was the fact that my anger was pushed deep inside of me.

As I learned how to box with her, I started to create healing and released images of me punching out of the basements I was locked in or the actual boxes I was locked into and finally freeing myself.

Therefore, the boxing sessions became more like therapy. During the childhood abuse, I wasn't allowed to display any form of resistance. Sometimes I even left the boxing sessions crying in my car or at home due to the powerful release I was experiencing.

Finally I was able to express anger and see myself as that child punching her way free. This was the work I needed to do! I give grace and gratitude for those boxing sessions and felt it was a missing healing piece for me. Today I have put away my gloves, yet still pursue my physical training with my trainer. I continue to enjoy gently pushing my body to new, physically stronger levels.

At times, confusion does rise inside my entire being. However, I remind myself that I am doing great. Relationships with romantic male partners remains a study for me. I made a promise to myself to further explore romantic relationships as my heart continues to pulsate to share life. A sense of confined, quiet loneliness sometimes surfaces, but I am content and know everything is in place and perfectly organized. As a fifty-year-old, I have never married, never lived with anyone, or had children. The baby I had named Little One was my child and will remain in my heart's wings of peace.

Today new ideas for projects to be manifested flood through my entire being. I have so many more words of silence and stillness to compose as well as new words to be unearthed and accepted into my composition of life. I have yet to present more authored books and courses, and new life lessons are revealed for me to receive and learn. I am learning how to do a headstand, dance with heels on to the Tango and Cha-Cha, and participate in just being me! I am thinking about taking singing lessons next!

I am enriched, happy, and filled with joy, surrounded by beautiful friends. And yes, I can really dance!

Remember to:

- Stay in love/grounded in balance.
- Step into power.
- Find your truth.
- Go through the gate.
- Have the little girl or boy go with you through the gate, as he or she represents the untouched, unwounded, and unscarred.
- Have the little girl or boy in your heart and holding your hand.

The little girl or boy finally gets to tell his or her story.

I do truly believe that, the further you step into the shadow or darkness, the higher in love and light you can transcend to. Then you realize more about life, and you can further explore love, peace, and stillness.

> *If I ever become a Saint—I will surely be one of*
> *"darkness." I will continually be absent from Heaven*
> *to light the light of those in darkness on earth.*
>
> —Mother Teresa of Calcutta

Today I am more than ready to continue to speak out publicly in any forum. I am informing people about this type of abuse and giving enthusiasm and hope for healing and transformation, which is so vital. My passion is to facilitate conferences, small or large; teach classes for social agencies; and speak to medical professionals, educational institutes, therapists and/or survivors. I offer individual care and support.

> *Have I performed my duty as a survivor? Have I transmitted all I was able to? Too much, perhaps? Too little perhaps?*
>
> —Ellie Wiesel (writer, professor, and Holocaust survivor)

I have written an entire body of work based on satanic abuse, which I am making available to you (www.feelingfree.ca). I did not intend to create a literary manifesto of tried-and-true theories and concepts, but to bring to light the raw foundation of this abuse. It is my sincere aspiration that my writing will aid in your personal processing or help reveal more awareness through the informed content in these documents. The purpose is to expose the amount of information that I have provided, all gained from my own lived experiences. This sojourn of the healing process and releasing can be passed on to assist others. That is my intention. I freed myself through the tangled knots of silence. Now I am talking!

The series of these documents in booklet format includes various topics as follows:

- "Exposing the Satanic Cult and Abuse"
- "Deprogramming Satanic Programmes"
- "How to Balance Your Life as You Heal"
- "Addendum of Hope"

- "Sexual Intimacy and Healing—The Unspoken Voice"
- "Healing Words and Passages for Satanic Abuse Survivors"
- "Breaking Free from the Illusion"
- "365 Day Healing Pages"

The first document, *"Exposing the Satanic Cult and Abuse,"* is a three hundred-page book that exposes in great detail the ritualistic activities and ceremonies. This is an account of what happens from fetus stage until around the age of sixteen years. All of the documents are directed specifically toward females. This material is raw to read, blunt, and clear, and you can actually see the patterns of satanic programs in their ritualistic schedules. Included are the types of music they use, the words, symbols, and locations.

This information would be most helpful for therapists to read of what you might hear when working with survivors or survivors seeking confirmation of their personal memories. I do strongly suggest that, if you are a survivor, you read this document along with a supporter.

The book *Deprogramming Satanic Programmes* includes a small sampling of twenty-five programs that satanists attempt to program into you physically, emotionally, mindfully, and energetically through all of your senses. The tools of how to deprogram these programs is described within this document. I also discuss post-hypnotic suggestions and how to recognize these and deprogram them.

Again, if you are a survivor, I would advise you to have a support person with you as you read the pages in this book, as the contents may be triggering. Be at peace and listen to your own truth.

I only come from the experience I experienced and inform you of what worked for me in reshaping my life. These tools and words in these books and booklets were designed to offer you help in any way possible.

This next booklet *How to Balance Your Life As You Heal* is perhaps one of the most important pieces of information in this series. When I was having so many memory flashbacks and feeling so hurt and in so much pain, it was difficult to maintain a balanced, regular life. I required constant and consistent support from several therapists and supporters in order to remain stable and alive. If you are seeking balance as a survivor, this booklet outlines ideas and suggestions that may provide you with some peace. What I learned is to do a bit at a time, to slow down my life in order to process everything. This helped me.

Additionally, *The Addendum of Hope* provides encouragement with several sections dedicated to all aspects of your life. There is hope in living your life free from this hurt. This is elegantly written with words that will dissolve into your heart.

Sexual intimacy is hard to speak about for survivors, and so I needed to write *Sexual Intimacy and Healing—The Unspoken Voice*. It contains carefully written material about sexual intimacy and the impact of satanic abuse upon sexual activity. I designed a questionnaire I call "Begin Gently," comprised of thirty questions that I asked myself several times throughout my healing journey. It addresses everything about sexual intimacy, feelings/no feelings, orgasm, touch, and other issues concerning satanic programs relating to sexual activity.

I was in a relationship during the fifteen years of therapy, but living apart during this time. I thank him for being patient and loving me through this. Many flashbacks or memories of abuse flooded through me during our sexual activity. I felt scared and sick to my stomach, and then I would dissociate or numb out. It got to a point whereby having sex was difficult, but it was a venue for releasing the memories.

Eventually the flashbacks stopped, and I was able to feel safe, sensual, and beautiful in sexual activity. It is complex, yet through this healing, this poem, "Stoning Tears," swept through me. Even though this relationship ended in severe pain and further hurt for me to sort out and heal, I am grateful for him loving me through the fifteen years of recovery as best as he knew how. He needed to be released from me and I from him.

"Stoning Tears" (1997)

Blackness of imagery smothers sensuality.

Stoning tears kill the soul, the heart.

Madness oozes from deep, wounded pores.

Kisses become bruising.

Touch hurts, aches the skin.

Hatred, anger, pushing, screaming.

Fragmented, separated self.

A warm soul approaches in whisper,

Understanding, love surrounding.

Strong, tender kisses remove the stones.

Bruises heal.

Touch recreates sensuality.

Love—UNITED SELF.

The next booklet is small but powerful. *"Healing Words in Passages for Satanic Abuse Survivors"* encompasses words and phrases to help a survivor move forward, one step at a time.

During my recovery, there really wasn't anything on this topic to read. I felt it important to write this little booklet that was specifically written for survivors. It provides a tiny nudge using language that may be important for someone to just take one step at a time into moving forward to freedom and into a better life.

In the beginning stages of healing, I quickly learned that I had a strong mind as well as being a strong person intellectually. This happens naturally when trauma is prevalent in children. Emotions shut down, leaving the mind in control. Needless to say, I bought over three hundred books on self-development during my fifteen years of healing. I felt the need to read about how to live in love and to be at peace. I recognized that learning to be kind to myself was vital.

What essentially happened was I became obsessively interested in not only healing but the self-development industry. I couldn't get enough of alluring quotes or reading about people's own courageous stories of awakening. Some of my favorite books and materials I make reference to are in the back of this book.

> " *I have been a seeker and still am but I stopped asking the books and the stars. I started listening to the teaching of my soul.* "
>
> —Rumi (poet)

The booklet *Breaking Free from the Illusion* is "moving from believing you are damaged to knowing you are whole, to allowing your true self to shine through … and learning that 'they' no longer have power over You!"

You can read about how satanic programming and abuse tries to convince you to live in fear, which is illusion. Once you recognize that you are created from love and that everything else outside of this is false, that's when a shift or transformation will happen.

There were times when I was believing God was punishing me because I was raised in this abuse. However, there was a reason, purpose, and plan for all of this to happen. Today I no longer believe I was being punished. There is a higher purpose in everything we do. Shifting through the messy feelings and being awkward and sloppy in releasing these feelings was just the way it was. This particular booklet asks the questions: What are your dreams, hopes, and wishes? What direction and path in life would you like to journey into now?

> " *My Future starts when I wake up every morning . . . Every day I find something creative to do with my life.* "
>
> —Miles Davis (jazz musician)

Move and shift into the direction of your dreams. You can achieve this and more. I promise you! If I can do this, you can do it too.

The last booklet I created is called *"365 Daily Healing Pages for Satanic Survivors,"* and I love this book. It is three hundred pages packed full of healing words of encouragement and reassurance.

For each day of the year, it contains a paragraph that will connect to every part of you. There is a "Day of Reaching Out," "Day of Grace and Glory," "Day of The Energy of Life," and others. By reading a daily page, you will begin to enjoy life and be present *now*. It's time to live!

When I first started this journey of healing, I found this poem, and it spoke to me. I rediscovered it recently when I was writing this book and believe the unknown author was a survivor of satanic abuse because her experiences are mirrored as mine. I would like to personally title the poem "I Survived."

"I Survived"

I am a woman who, as a child, was taught hate for all life.

I am a woman who loves deeply.

I am a woman who, as a child, had electrodes placed on her body,

and was locked in a box.

I am a woman who is free.

I am a woman who, as a child, was filmed in her sexual torture and saw death.

I am a woman who believes in her rightful place in this world and is fully alive.

I am a woman so full of light, sometimes I do know just how I survived.

Unknown

We are living in an era of coming together, dropping old, painful patterns, and releasing destructive thoughts and unhealthy relationships. Being aware is the first key to our movement toward stillness. We are all being called to action. It is a time to step up. It is time to awaken, to open your eyes, expose, release, and love. Let's support each other.

Turning the Darkness Outward and Exposing the Living Light from Deep Within

This isn't about me.
I walked through this darkness in order to say to you:
Stand proud and strong.
Listen to your truth.
Trust yourself as best as you can.
Find "your" truth.
Stand in joy.
Step out of the illusion
Believe in yourself and others.
Step into your power.
Go through the darkness into the Light.
There is hope
You can and must do it!

This book is gifted and further dedicated to those who seek freedom through speaking their truth. You are being heard and loved.

Reflections

" *Someone is enjoying shade today because someone planted a tree a long time ago.* "

—Warren Buffett (philanthropist)

Reflections

“ *My socks may not match, but my feet are always warm.* ”

—Maureen McCullough (actor)

Reflections

> *Do exactly what your "yeah-but" says You shouldn't. Write that novel. Adopt a puppy. Resist oppression. Keep the "yeah" and Kick the "butt"!*

—Martha Beck (life coach)

Reflections

> " *There are no great deeds; there are just small deeds done with great love.* "
>
> —Mother Teresa

Reflections

" *What lies behind us and what lies before us are tiny matters compared to what lies within us.* "

—Ralph Waldo Emerson (philosopher)

Reflections

> " *I'm not telling you, You are good enough. I am telling you,*
> *You are complete and perfect before even the birth of time.* "
>
> —Mooji (spiritual teacher)

Reflections

❝ *Follow your bliss.* ❞

—Joseph Campbell (teacher and writer)

Profound Gratitude

I am profoundly blessed to have experienced the depths of loving care and healing from so many compassionate and grace-filled people. I believe these individuals are Angels in human form. People show up just when you need them. I truly know this to be true.

I know their kindness and hugs held me in love through so much of my recovery journey. Many still hold my hand through the continued life's journey. I love all of you!

Acknowledgements and thanks to the voices of those teachers quoted herein. I place my hands on my heart and give each and every one of these supporters grace and my profound gratitude.

Resources to Order by Sarah

www.feelingfree.ca

The following material is mentioned inside the contents of the book.

- Exposing the Satanic Cult and Abuse

- Deprogramming Satanic Programmes

- How to Balance Your Life as You Heal

- Addendum of Hope

- Sexual Intimacy and Healing—The Unspoken Voice

- Healing Words and Passages for Satanic Abuse Survivors

- Breaking Free from the Illusion

- 365 Day Healing Pages

Suggested Readings

The Passion Test (Hudson Street Press, 2007) by Janet Attwood and Chris Attwood

Codependency No More (Hazelden Foundation, 1986) by Melody Beattie

Virus Of The Mind (Hay House, 1996) by Richard Brodie

Trust Your Vibes (Hay House, 2004) by Sonia Choquette

Soul Shifts (Hay House, 2015) by Dr. Barbara DeAngelis

Change Your Thoughts—Change Your Life (Hay House, 2007) by Dr. Wayne W. Dyer

The Shadow Effect (Harper One, 2010) by Debbie Ford, Deepak Chopra and Marianne Williamson

Man's Search For Meaning (Pocket Books, 1959) by Viktor Frankl

Power vs Force (Veritas Publishing, 1995) by David Hawkins

You Can Heal Your Life (Hay House, 1984) by Louise Hay

Loving What Is (Three Rivers Press, 2002) by Byron Katie

Beyond Fear (Council Oak Books, 1997) by Don Miguel Ruiz

The Four Agreements (Amber-Allen Publishing, 1997) by Don Miguel Ruiz

Transformation Soup (Simon Schuster, 2000) by SARK

Mind Programming (Hay House, 2009) by Eldon Taylor

A New Earth (A. Plume Book, 2005) by Eckhart Tolle

The Power of Now (Namaste Publishing, 1999) by Eckhart Tolle

Open Heart (Schocken Books, 2001) by Elie Wiesel

Printed in the United States
By Bookmasters